Pilgrim, Pastor, Friend

Excerpts from homilies and addresses by

Pope John Paul II

during his 1987 Pastoral Visit to the United States

Photographs by

**St. Petersburg Times
Arturo Mari
Daughters of St. Paul**

St. Paul Books & Media

ISBN 0-8198-5824-2

Copyright © 1987 by the Daughters of St. Paul

Printed in the U.S.A., by the Daughters of St. Paul
50 St. Paul's Ave., Boston, MA 02130

The Daughters of St. Paul are an international congregation of women religious serving the Church with the communications media.

CONTENTS

Miami ... 8
South Carolina ... 22
New Orleans ... 26
San Antonio ... 38
Phoenix ... 54
Los Angeles ... 64
Monterey ... 74
San Francisco ... 84
Detroit ... 94

ACKNOWLEDGMENT

The Daughters of St. Paul wish to express their grateful appreciation to the St. Petersburg Times for access to their transparencies of the Holy Father's visit—from which the majority of these photos have been selected.

Miami

It is a great joy for me once again to be in your country, and I thank you for your warm welcome. I am deeply grateful to you all.

I come to proclaim the Gospel of Jesus Christ to all those who freely choose to listen to me; to tell again the story of God's love in the world; to spell out once more the message of human dignity, with its inalienable human rights and its inevitable human duties.

Like so many before me coming to America and to this very city of Miami, I come as a pilgrim: a pilgrim in the cause of justice and peace and human solidarity—striving to build up the one human family.

I come here as a pastor—the pastor of the Catholic Church, to speak and pray with the Catholic people.

I come as a friend—a friend of America and of all Americans: Catholics, Orthodox, Protestants and Jews, people of every religion, and all men and women of good will.

September 10-11, 1987

I am grateful to you, my brother priests, for your welcome of fraternal love. I express my gratitude for your ministry, for your perseverance, for your faith and love, for the fact that you are striving to live the priesthood....

I have come to you because I want all distances to be bridged, so that together we may grow and become ever more truly a communion of faith, hope and love. I affirm you in the good gifts you have received and in the generous response you have made to the Lord and his people, and I encourage you to become more and more like Jesus Christ—the Eternal High Priest, the Good Shepherd.

St. Petersburg Times

St. Petersburg Times

I express my special thanks to the President of the United States, who honors me by his presence here today.

My cordial greetings and good wishes go to all the people of this land. I thank you for opening your hearts to me and for supporting me by your prayers. I assure you of my own prayers.

Arturo Mari

Arturo Mari

St. Petersburg Times

St. Petersburg Times

Arturo Mari

St. Petersburg Times

St. Petersburg Times

The United States was founded by people who came to these shores, often as religious refugees. Among these millions of immigrants there was a large number of Catholics and Jews. The same *basic religious principles* of freedom and justice, of equality and moral solidarity, affirmed in the *Torah* as well as in the *Gospel*, were in fact reflected in the high human ideals and in the protection of universal rights found in the United States. Jews and Catholics have contributed to the success of the American experiment in religious freedom, and, in this unique context, have given to the world a vigorous form of interreligious dialogue between our two ancient traditions. For those engaged in this dialogue, I pray: May God bless you and make you strong for his service!

St. Petersburg Times

Arturo Mari

The civic community and the Church in Southern Florida have, time after time, opened their arms to immigrants and refugees. Be sure that as often as you did it for them, you did it for Christ.

I assure you of the Church's particular concern for those who leave their native countries out of suffering and desperation. The frequent repetition of this experience is one of the saddest phenomena of our century. Yet it has often been accompanied by hope and heroism and new life. Here in Miami I know there are many who, in the face of distress, have been faithful to the Gospel and the law of God. Like others who have remained faithful to Christ and his Church in time of oppression, you must guard and protect your Catholic faith as you now live your lives in freedom.

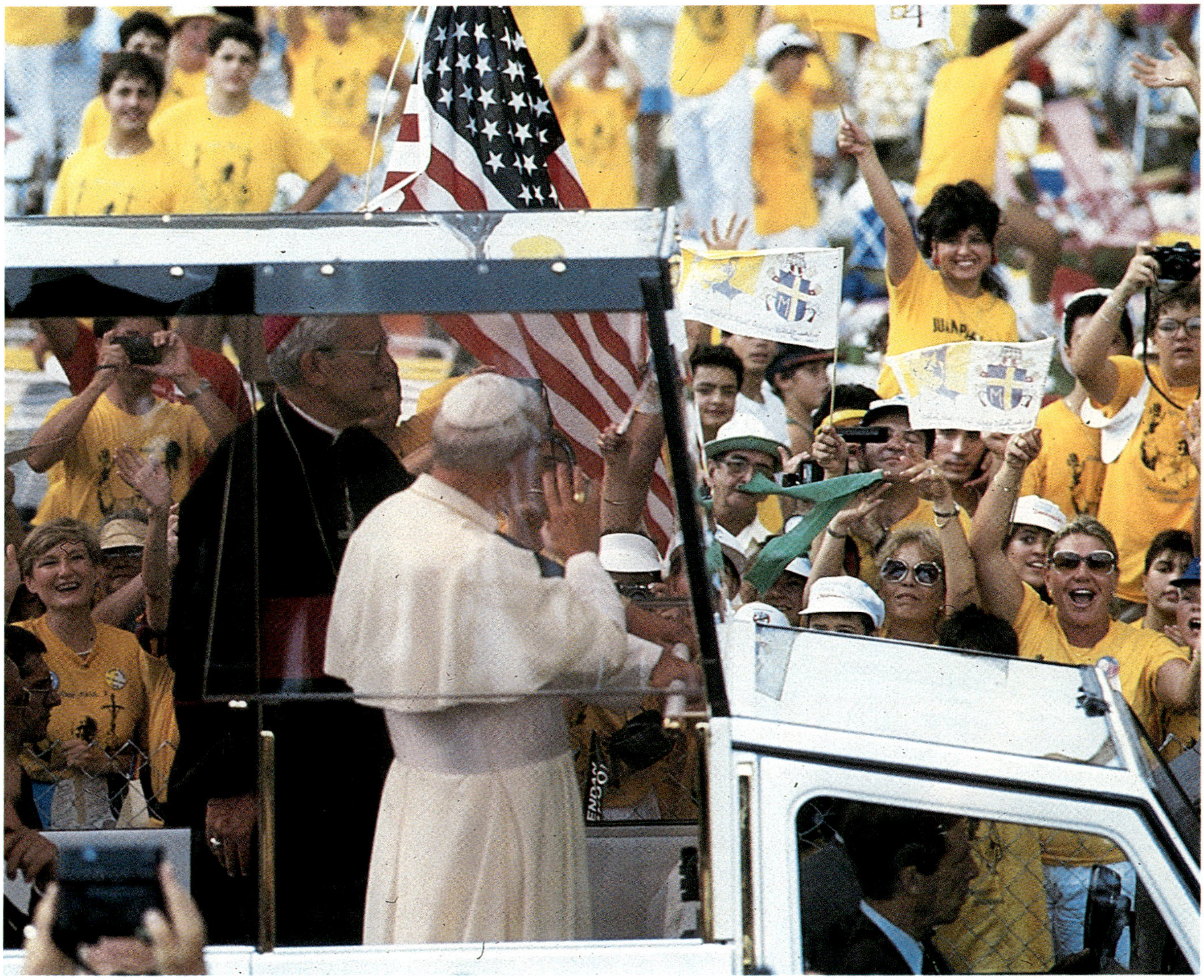

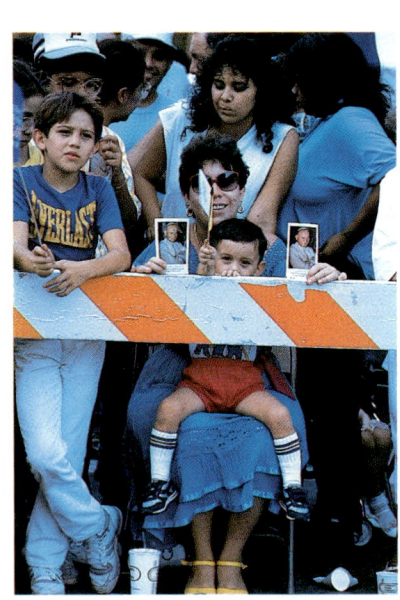

St. Petersburg Times

St. Petersburg Times

20

South Carolina

The Scriptures are dear to all of us. They are one of the greatest treasures we share. In the Sacred Scriptures and in the deeds of divine mercy which they narrate, God our Father, out of the abundance of his love, speaks to us as his children and lives among us.

Today this stadium has resounded with passages from Holy Scripture bearing on the reality of the family. Marriage and the family are sacred realities. In God's plan the marriage covenant between a man and a woman becomes the image and symbol of the covenant which unites God and his people.

Contemporary society has a splendid need of the witness of couples who persevere in their union, as an eloquent "sign" in our human condition of the steadfastness of God's love. Day after day Christian married couples are called to open their hearts ever more to the Holy Spirit whose power never fails, and who enables them to love each other as Christ has loved us.

From such love Christian families are born. In them children are welcomed as a splendid gift of God's goodness, and they are educated in the essential values of human life, learning above all that "man is more precious for what he is than for what he has."

Brothers and sisters: to the extent that God grants us to grow in Christian unity, let us work together to offer strength and support to families, on whom the well-being of society depends, and on whom our Churches and Ecclesial Communities depend.

September 11, 1987

Arturo Mari

DSP

St. Petersburg Times

DSP

24

Let us give thanks to God and rejoice in this fellowship! And let us commit ourselves to the great task which Jesus himself urges upon us: to go forward along the path of Christian reconciliation and unity....

Arturo Mari

Arturo Mari

DSP

DSP

New Orleans

It is with the truth of Jesus, dear young people, that you must face the great questions in your lives, as well as the practical problems. The world will try to deceive you about many things that matter: about your faith, about pleasure and material things, about the dangers of drugs. And at one stage or another the false voices of the world will try to exploit your human weakness by telling you that life has no meaning at all for you. The supreme theft in your lives would be if they succeeded in robbing you of hope. They will try, but they will not succeed if you hold fast to Jesus and his truth.... You will be invincible in hope: "in Christ Jesus our hope."

September 11-12, 1987

Arturo Mari

St. Petersburg Times

St. Petersburg Times

DSP

DSP

St. Petersburg Times

Jesus' message applies to all the areas of life. He reveals to us the truth of our lives and all aspects of this truth. Jesus tells us that the purpose of our freedom is to say "yes" to God's plan for our lives. What makes our "yes" so important is that we say it freely.

I proclaim to you again Jesus Christ: the way, and the truth and the life—your way, your truth and your life.

There is no black Church, no white Church, no American Church; but there is and must be, in the one Church of Jesus Christ, a home for blacks, whites, Americans, every culture and race.

Dear young people of America, in the Church there are many different gifts. There is room for many different cultures and ways of doing things. But there is no room in the Church for selfishness. There is no room in the world for selfishness. It destroys the meaning of life; it destroys the meaning of love; it reduces the human person to a subhuman level.... You young people must change society by your lives of justice and fraternal love. It is not just a question of your own country, but of the whole world.

Arturo Mari

37

St. Petersburg Times

San Antonio

The Church has always proclaimed a love of preference for the poor. Perhaps the language is new, but the reality is not. Nor has the Church taken a narrow view of poverty and the poor. Poverty, certainly, is often a matter of material deprivation. But it is also a matter of spiritual impoverishment, the lack of human liberties, and the result of any violation of human rights and human dignity. There is a very special and pitiable form of poverty: the poverty of selfishness, the poverty of those who have and will not share, of those who could be rich by giving but choose to be poor by keeping everything they have. These people too need help.

The Christian view is that human beings are to be valued for what they are, not for what they have. In loving the poor and serving those in whatever need, the Church seeks above all to respect and heal their human dignity. The aim of Christian solidarity and service is to defend and promote, in the name of Jesus Christ, the dignity and fundamental human rights of every person. The Church "bears witness to the fact that this dignity cannot be destroyed, whatever the situation of poverty, scorn, rejection or powerlessness to which a human being has been reduced. She shows her solidarity with those who do not count in a society by which they are rejected spiritually and sometimes even physically. She is particularly drawn with maternal affection toward those children who, through human wickedness, will never be brought forth from the womb to the light of day, as also for the elderly, alone and abandoned. The special option for the poor, far from being a sign of particularism or sectarianism, manifests the universality of the Church's being and mission."

September 13, 1987

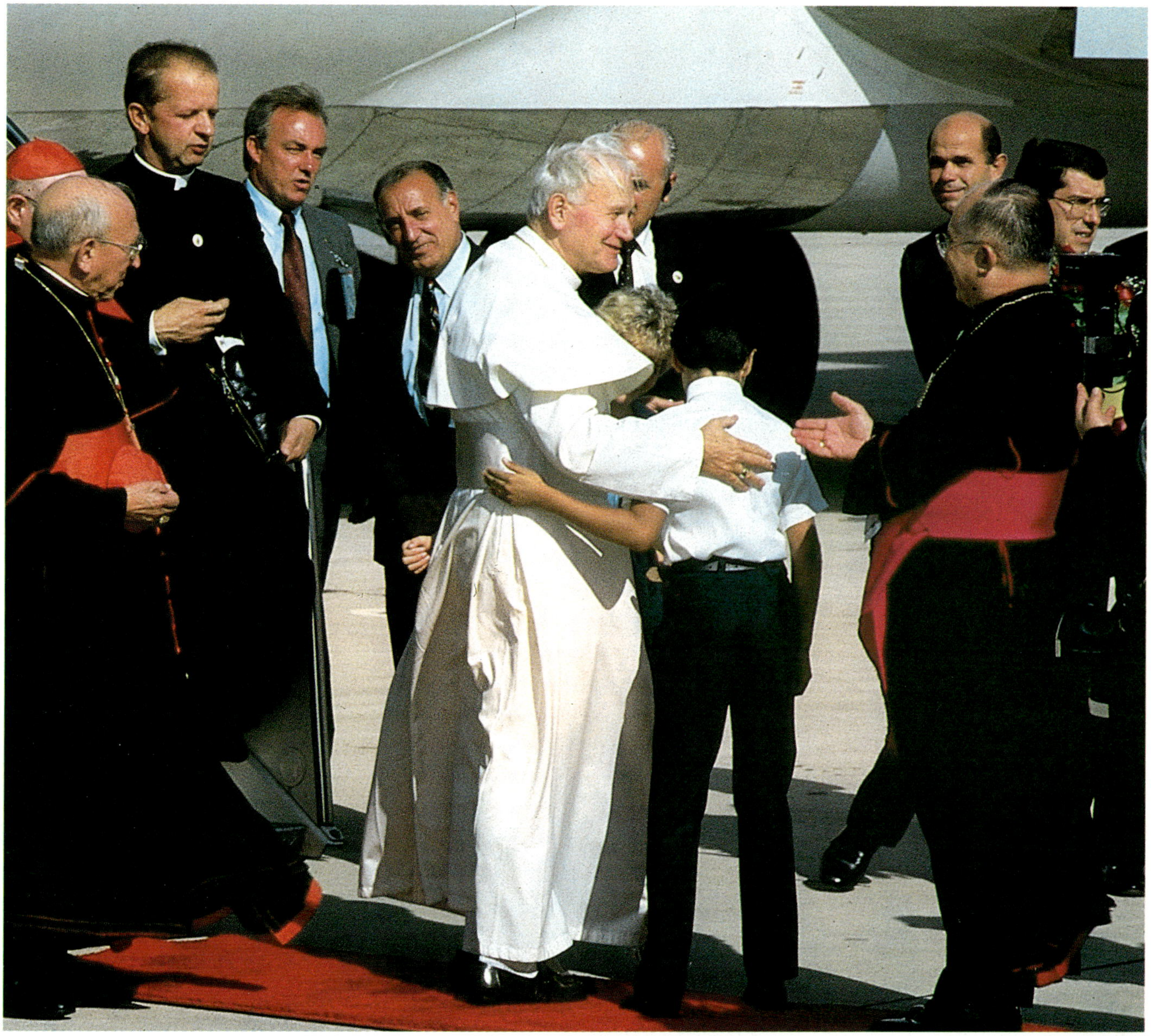

St. Petersburg Times

Like Mary, we too have been given the gift of God's grace, even though we have not received its fullness. Like Mary, we are called to respond, to be open to God's word, to be generous in saying "yes" to God. For us this means doing God's will, living according to his commandments, serving our neighbor, avoiding sin. In other words, with Mary we must respond with love to God's love.

Let us turn then to Mary whom we honor...under her special title of Our Lady of Guadalupe.

DSP

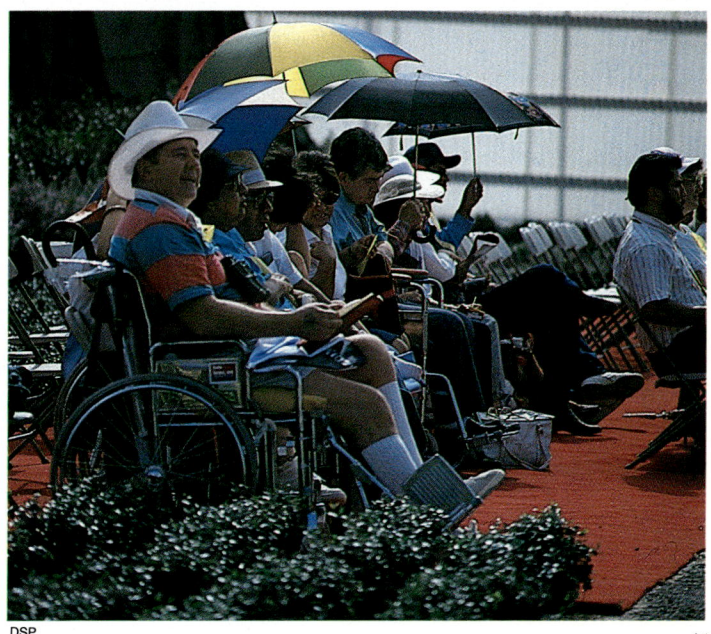

Only the human person, created in the image and likeness of God, is capable of raising a hymn of praise and thanksgiving to the Creator.

DSP

DSP

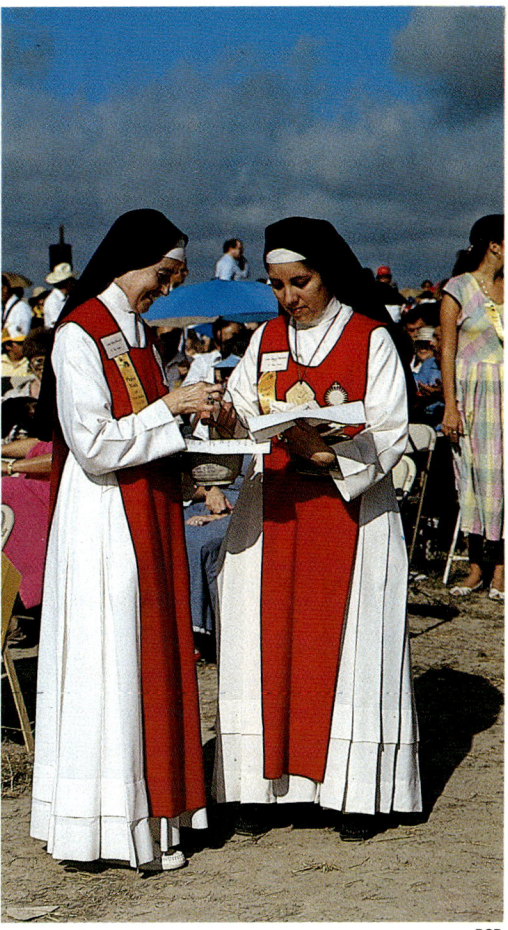

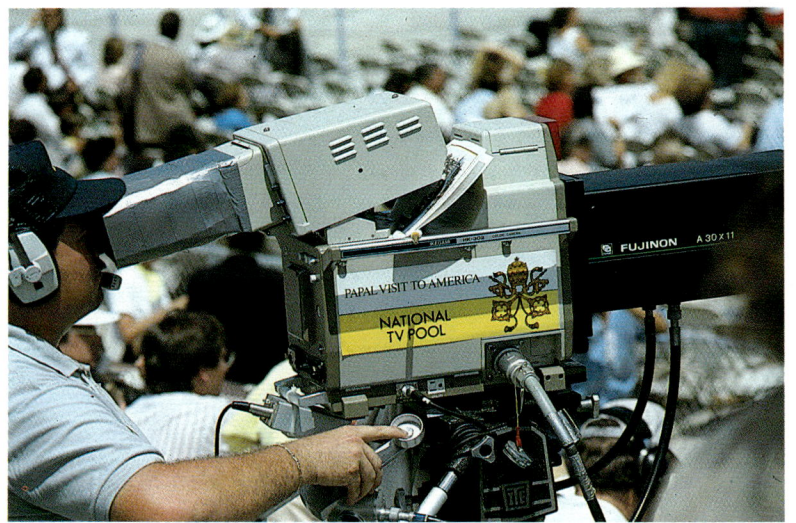

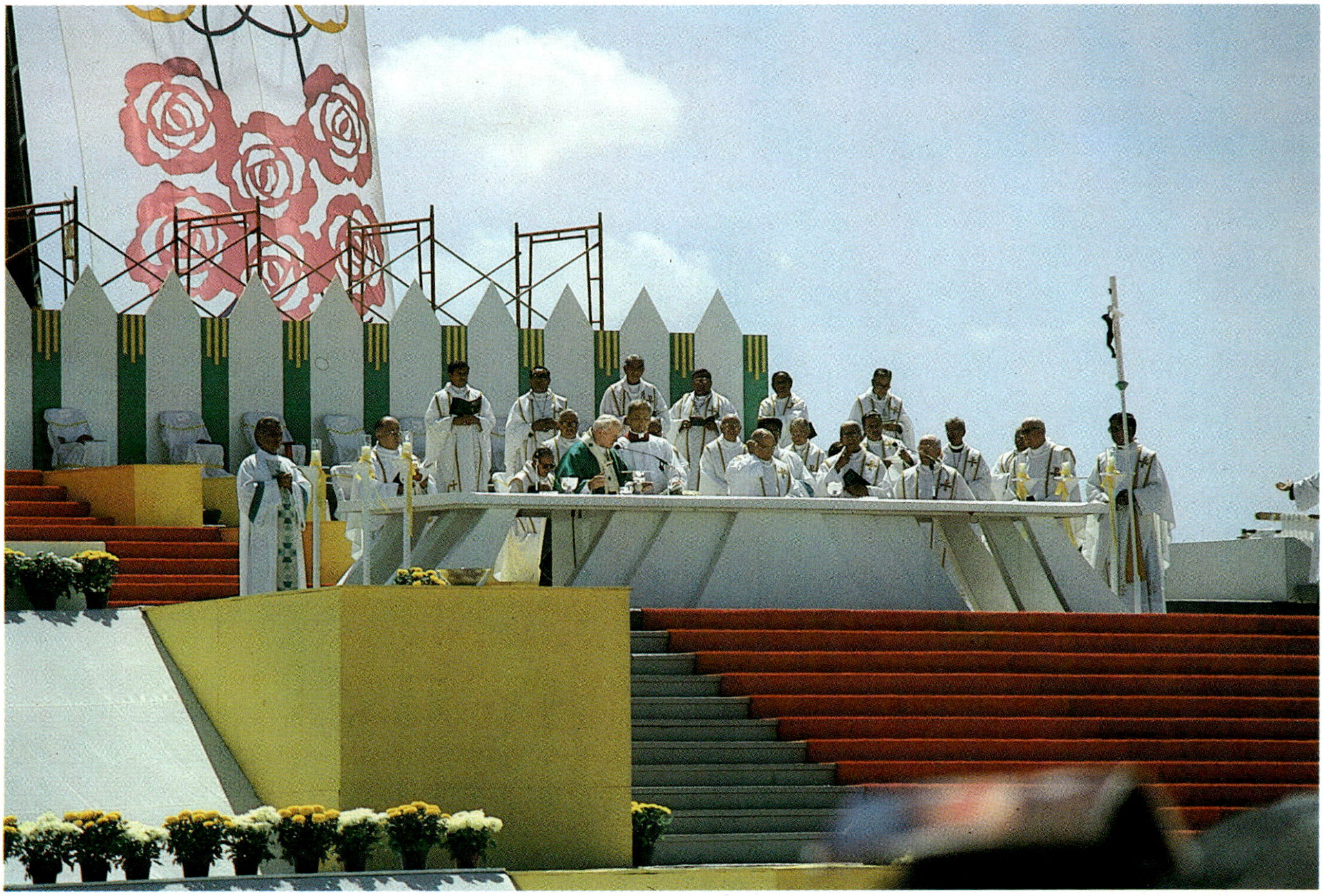
DSP

Arturo Mari

DSP

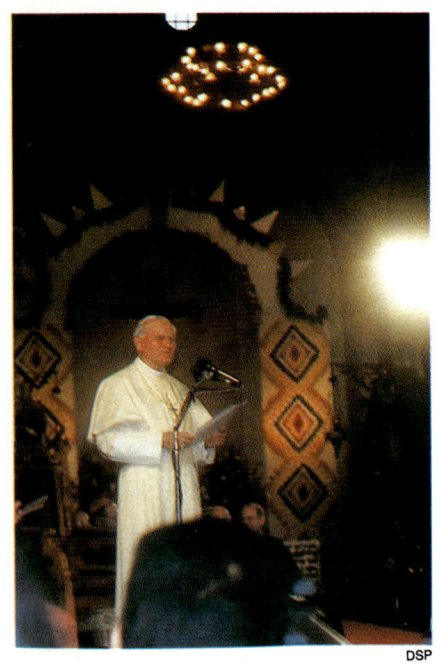

I am happy to know that the number of Hispanic priests and men and women religious is growing. But many more are needed. Young Hispanics: is Christ calling you? Hispanic families: are you willing to give your sons and daughters to the Church's service? Do you ask the Lord to send laborers into his harvest? Christ needs Hispanic laborers for the great harvest of the Hispanic community and the whole Church.

St. Petersburg Times

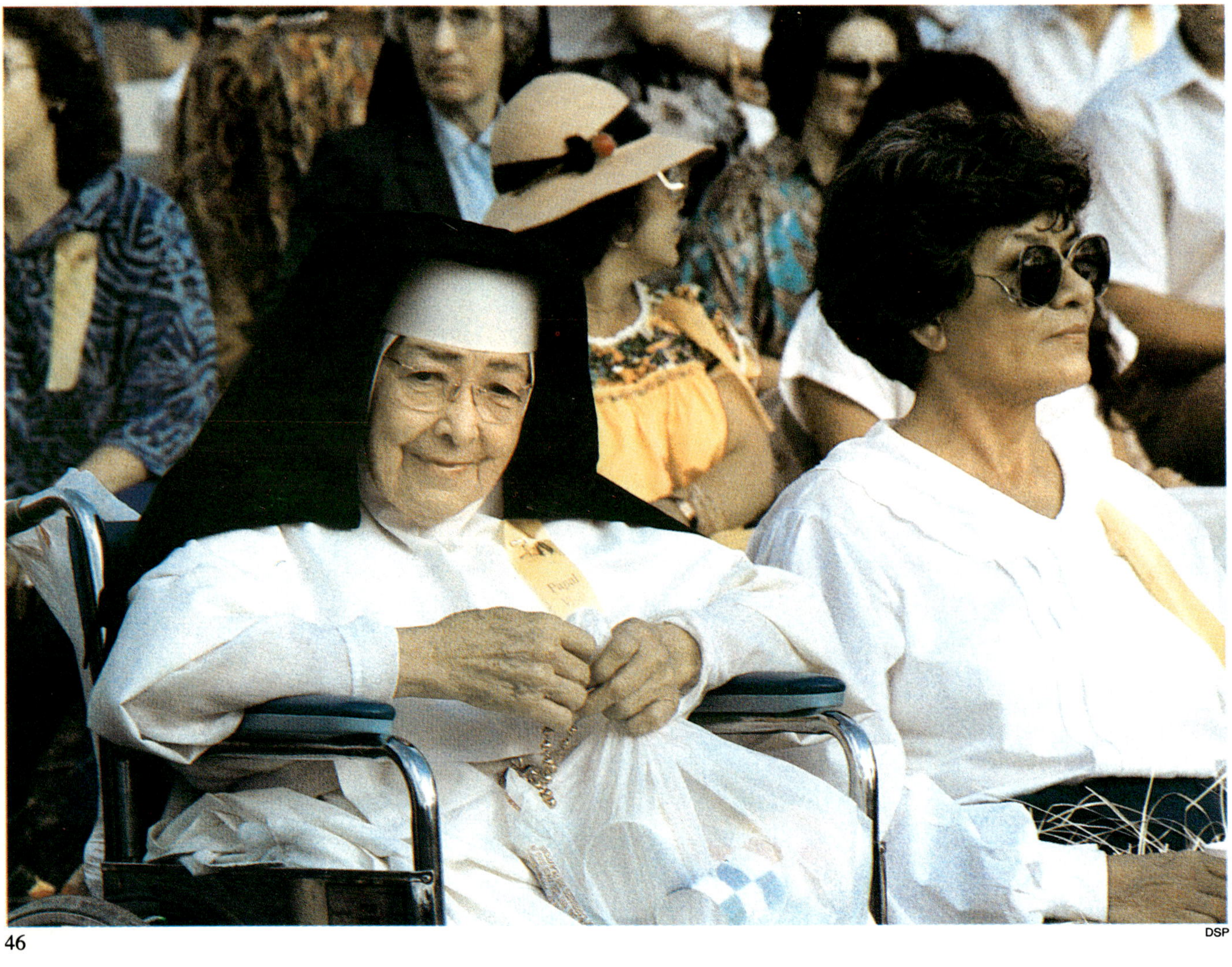

DSP

48

Those of you of Hispanic descent—so numerous, so long present in this land, so well equipped to respond—are called to hear the word of Christ and take it to heart: "I give you a new commandment, love one another. Such as my love has been for you, so must your love be for each other." The Hispanic community also has to respond to its own needs, and to show generous and effective solidarity among its own members. I urge you to hold fast to your Christian faith and traditions, especially in defense of the family.

St. Petersburg Times

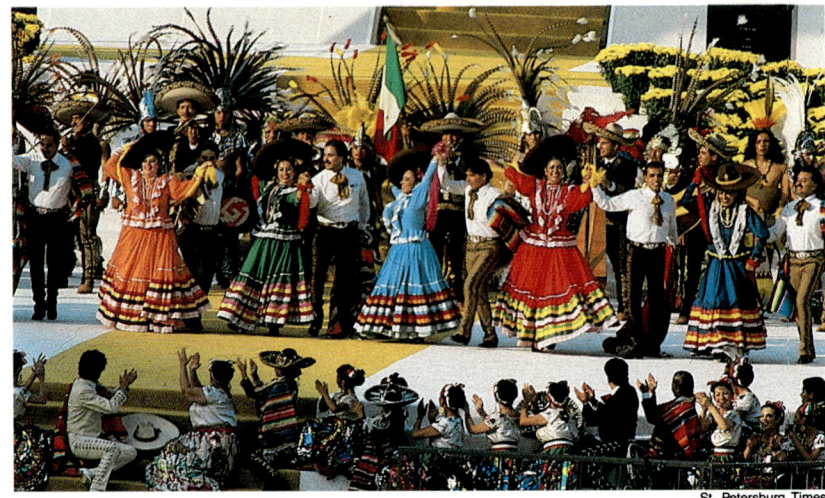

This land is a crossroads, standing at the border of two great nations, and experiencing both the enrichment and the complications which arise from this circumstance. You are thus a symbol and a kind of laboratory, testing America's commitment to her founding moral principles and human values.

DSP

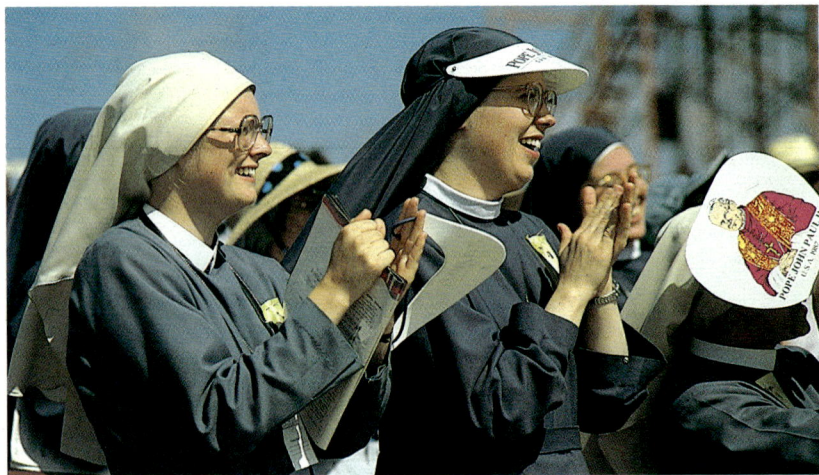

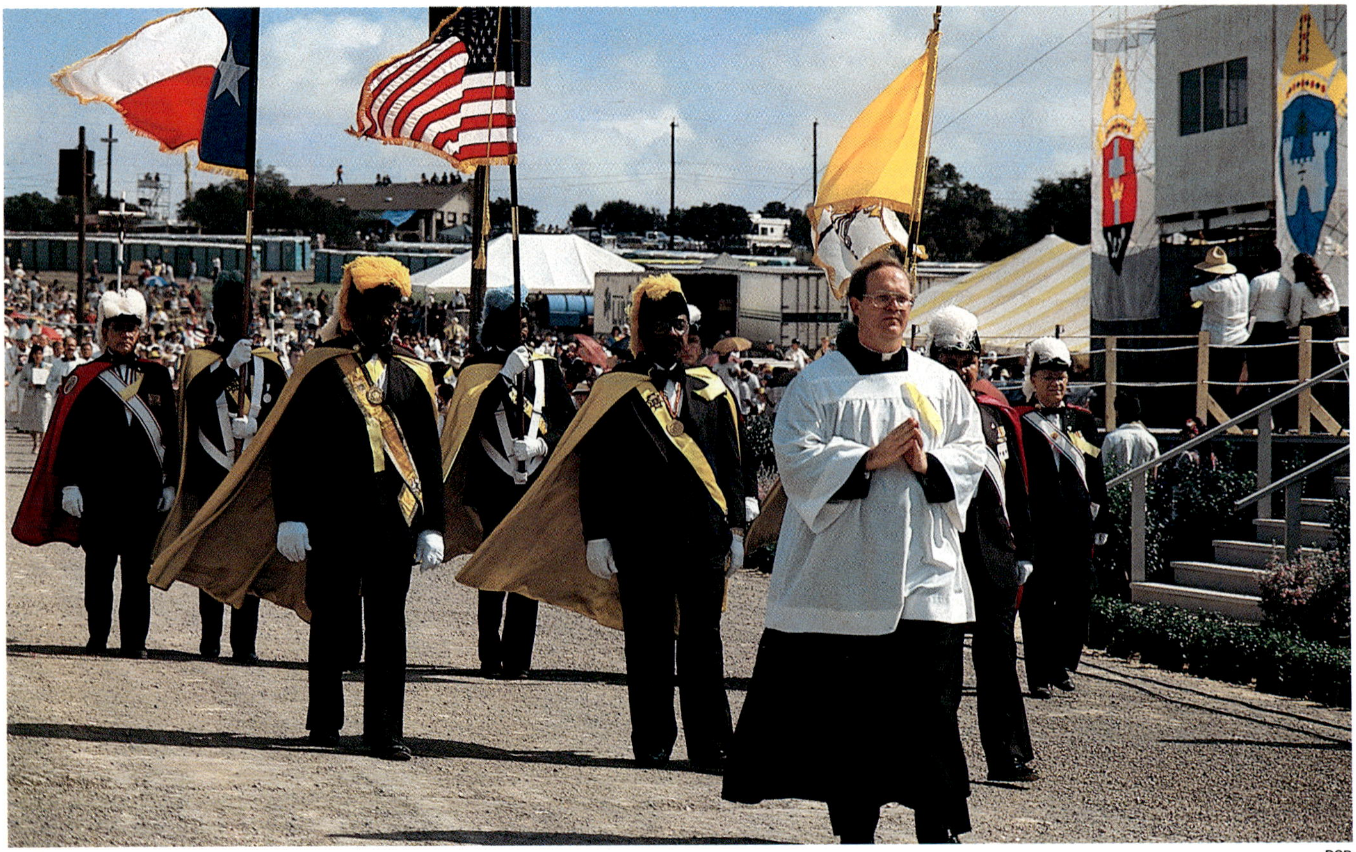

DSP

St. Petersburg Times

St. Petersburg Times

DSP

51

I appeal to you, the Catholic families of the United States: be true families—united, reconciled and loving; and be true Catholic families—prayerful communities living the Catholic faith, open to the needs of others, taking part fully in the life of the parish and of the Church at large.

Arturo Mari

...w Jesus came to serve ... signs of his mission was ... to the poor, and he showed in ... love for the poor and suffering. We are con... ...ore, that if we follow the teaching and exam... ...ur beloved Lord, we shall find ourselves more closely united with one another, especially the needy, and we shall experience that transcendent dimension of life which can only be attained in union with God.

Concern for the sick and suffering is part of the Church's life and mission. The Church has always understood herself to be charged by Christ with the care of the poor, the weak, the defenseless, the suffering and those who mourn. This means that those who alleviate suffering and seek to heal, also bear witness to the Christian view of suffering and to the meaning of life and death as taught by our Christian faith.

In every age of the Church, God makes his chosen ones "perfect through suffering," bringing them to the fullness of life and happiness by giving them on earth a share in the cross of Christ.

Christian life finds its whole meaning in love, but love does not exist for us without effort, discipline and sacrifice in every aspect of our life. We are willing to give in proportion as we love, and when love is perfect the sacrifice is complete. God so loved the world that he gave his only Son, and the Son so loved us that he gave his life for our salvation.

September 14, 1987

Arturo Mari

Arturo Mari

St. Petersburg Times

St. Petersburg Times

St. Petersburg Times

Arturo Mari

Arturo Mari

St. Petersburg Times

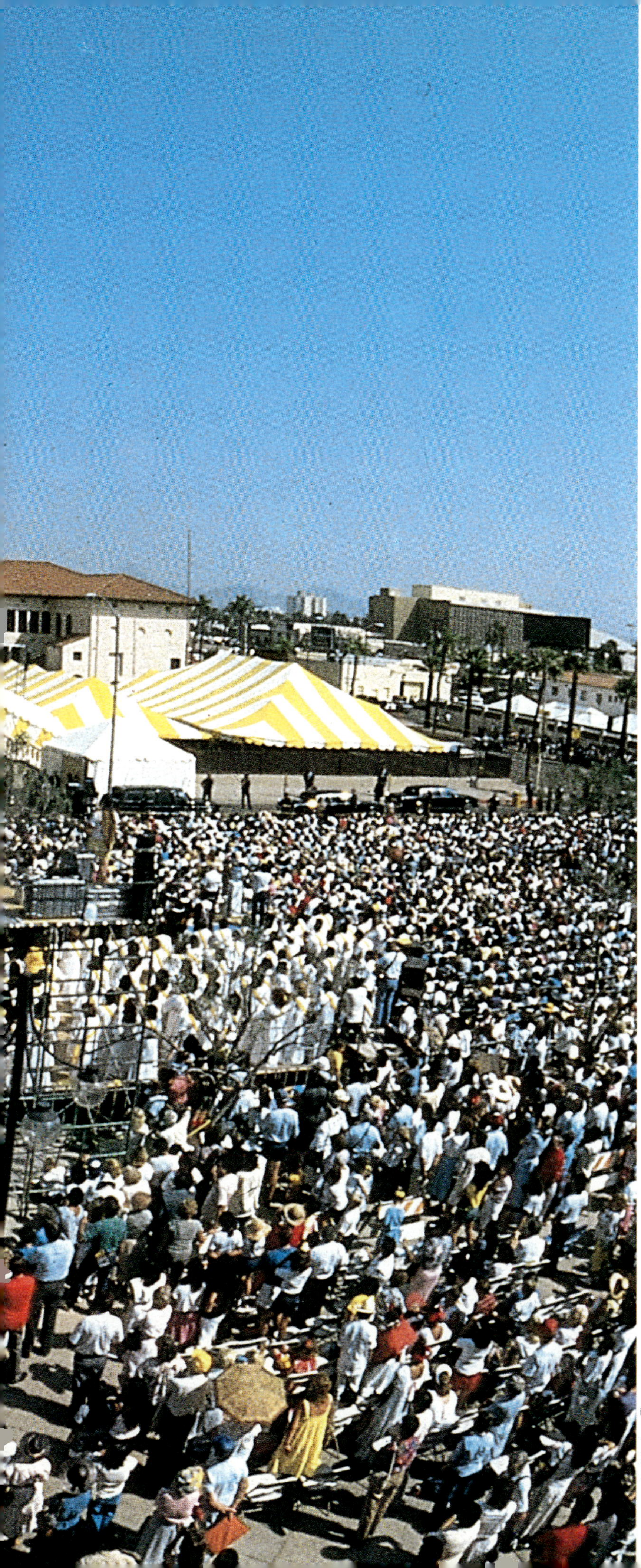

St. Petersburg Times

DSP

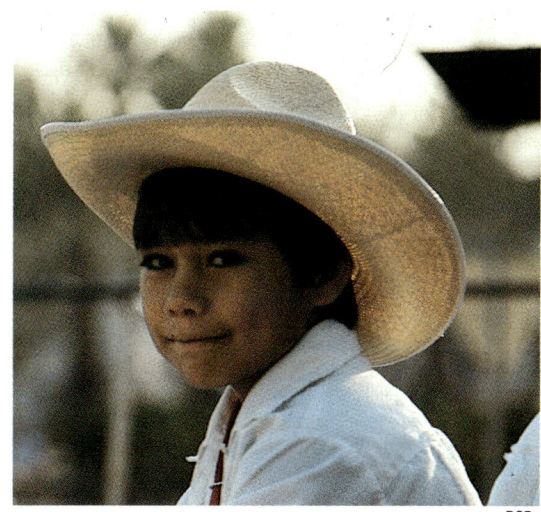

Today, people are realizing more and more clearly that we all belong to the one human family and are meant to walk and work together in mutual respect, understanding, trust and love. Within this family each people preserves and expresses its own identity and enriches others with its gifts of culture, tradition, customs, stories, song, dance, art and skills.

I encourage you, as native people belonging to the different tribes and nations...to preserve and keep alive your cultures, your languages, the values and customs which have served you well in the past and which provide a solid foundation for the future. The Gospel of Jesus Christ is at home in every people. It enriches, uplifts and purifies every culture. All of us together make up the People of God, the Body of Christ, the Church.

I wish to urge the local Churches to be truly "catholic" in their outreach to native peoples, and to show respect and honor for their culture and all their worthy traditions.

Arturo Mari

Arturo Mari

Arturo Mari

Los Angeles

Dear brothers and sisters, the name of Jesus, like the Word of God that he is, is a two-edged sword. It is a name that means salvation and life; it is a name that means a struggle and a cross, just as it did for him.

Dear people of this great Archdiocese of Los Angeles, with its many problems, its enormous challenges, and its immense possibilities for good: The name of Jesus is your life and your salvation. It is your pride and joy, and the pride and joy of your families and your parishes. In this name you find strength for your weaknesses and energy for daily Christian living. In your struggle against evil and the Evil One, and in your striving for holiness, the name of Jesus is the source of your hope, because in the name of Jesus you are invincible!

Continue, then, dear Catholic people of Los Angeles, to invoke this holy name of Jesus in your joys and your sorrows; continue to teach this name to your children so that they in turn can teach it to their children, until the Lord Jesus himself comes in glory to judge the living and the dead!

September 15-16, 1987

Arturo Mari

"[World Religions] share a common respect of and obedience to conscience, which teaches all of us to seek the truth, to love and serve all individuals and peoples, and therefore to make peace among individuals and among nations." Let us continue to seek peace for the human family: through prayer, since peace transcends our human efforts; through penance, since we have not always been "peacemakers"; through prophetic witness, since old divisions and social evils need to be challenged; and through constant initiatives on behalf of the rights of individuals and nations, and on behalf of justice everywhere. The fragile gift of peace will survive only if there is a concerted effort on the part of all.

St. Petersburg Times

Arturo Mari

Arturo Mari

Let us learn the virtue of compassion from her whose heart was pierced with a sword at the foot of the cross. It is the virtue that prompted the Good Samaritan to stop beside the victim on the road, rather than to continue on or to cross over to the other side. Whether it be the case of the person next to us or of distant peoples and nations, we must be Good Samaritans to all those who suffer. We must be the compassionate "neighbor" of those in need, not only when it is emotionally rewarding or convenient, but also when it is demanding and inconvenient. Compassion is a virtue we cannot neglect in a world in which the human suffering of so many of our brothers and sisters is needlessly increased by oppression, deprivation and underdevelopment—by poverty, hunger and disease. Compassion is also called for in the face of the spiritual emptiness and aimlessness that people can often experience amid material prosperity and comfort in developed countries such as your own. Compassion is a virtue that brings healing to those who bestow it, not only in this present life but in eternity: "Blessed are they who show mercy, mercy shall be theirs."

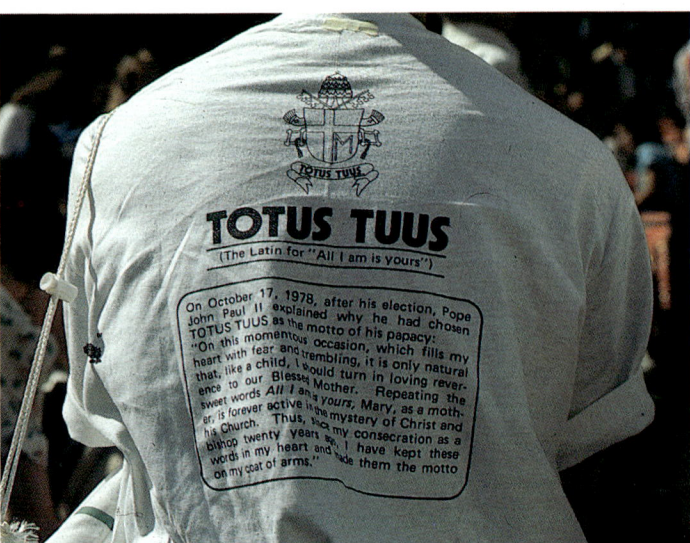

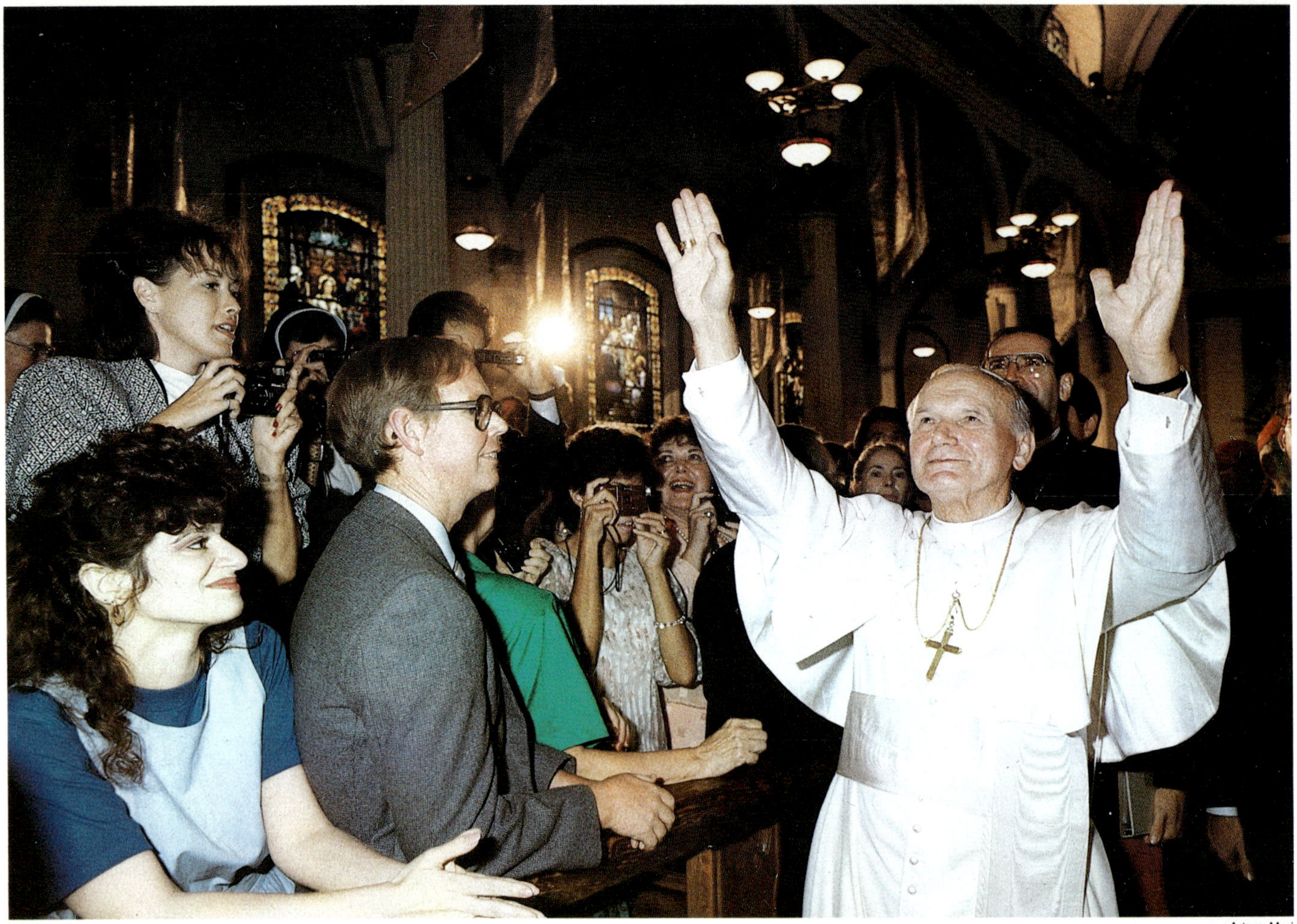

Arturo Mari

Dear young people of America, listen to Christ's voice. Do not be afraid. Open up your hearts to Christ. The deepest joy in life is the joy that comes from God and is found in Jesus Christ, the Son of God. He is the hope of the world. Jesus Christ is your hope and mine!

Arturo Mari

Arturo Mari

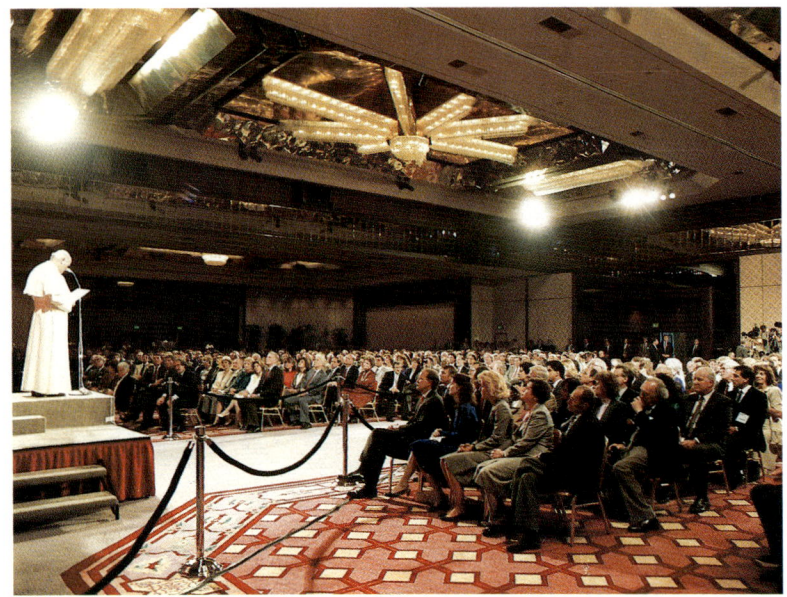

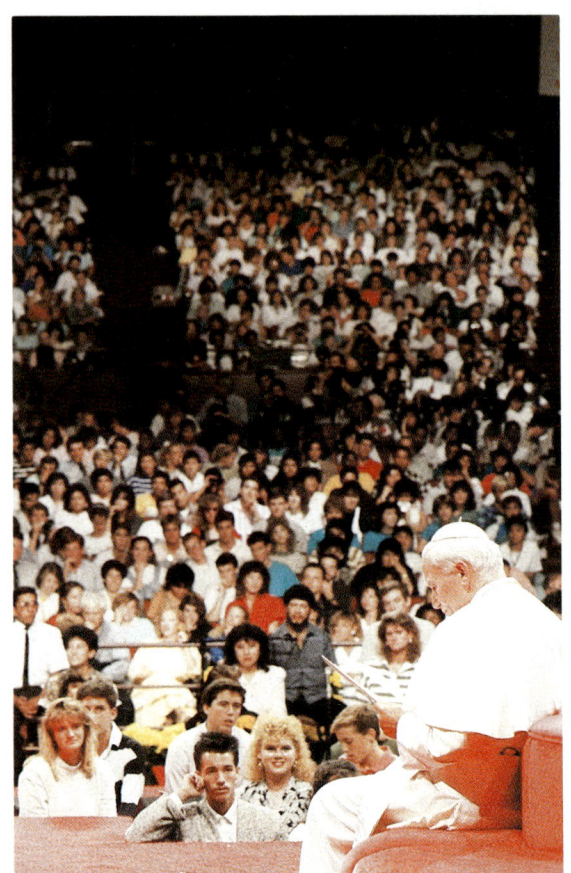

We cannot live without hope. We have to have some purpose in life, some meaning to our existence. We have to aspire to something. Without hope, we begin to die.

Hope comes from God, from our belief in God. People of hope are those who believe God created them for a purpose and that he will provide for their needs. They believe that God loves them as a faithful Father. Yes, God knows all our needs. He is the foundation for our hope.

DSP

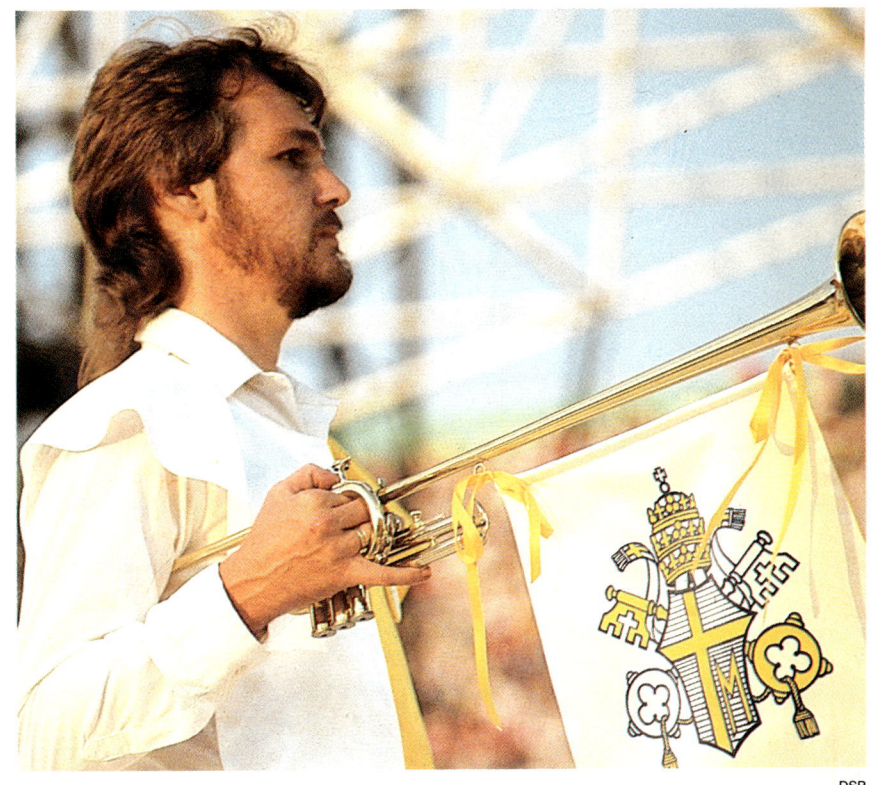

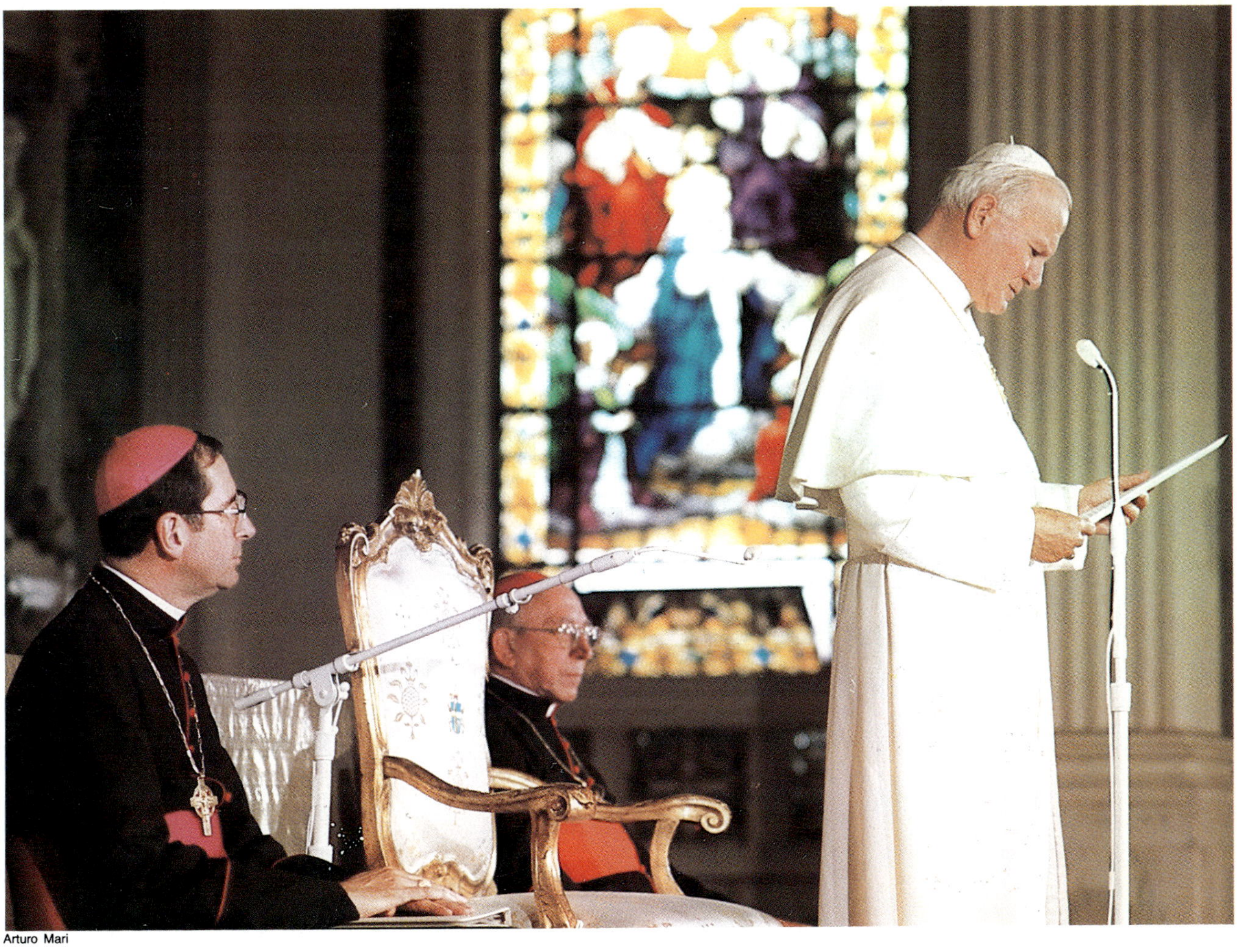

Arturo Mari

Monterey

Jesus teaches that the Reign of God is like the growth of the seed that a man scatters on the ground. Certainly, human activity is essential. Man "goes to bed and gets up every day...." He plants. And "when the crop is ready he wields the sickle." Even the rich valleys of California would produce nothing without human ingenuity and toil. But the word of God says that "the soil produces of itself first the blade, then the ear, finally the ripe wheat in the ear," as if to say: the growth of the wheat and its maturing, which greatly depends on the fertility of the soil, comes from the nature and vitality of creation itself. Consequently there is another source of growth: the One who is above nature and above the man who cultivates the earth.

In a sense, the Creator "hides himself" in this life-giving process of nature. It is the human person, with the help of intellect and faith, who is called to "discover" and "unveil" the presence of God and his action in all of creation: "So may your way be known upon earth; among all nations, your salvation."

September 17, 1987

Dear brothers and sisters: it is in the Eucharist that the fruits of our work—and all that is noble in human affairs—become an offering of the greatest value in union with the Sacrifice of Jesus Christ, our Lord and Savior. In fostering what is authentically human through our work and through deeds of justice and love, we set upon the altar of the Lord those elements which will be transformed into Christ: "Blessed are you, Lord, God of all creation. Through your goodness we have this bread to offer, which earth has given and human hands have made. It will become for us the bread of life."

St. Petersburg Times

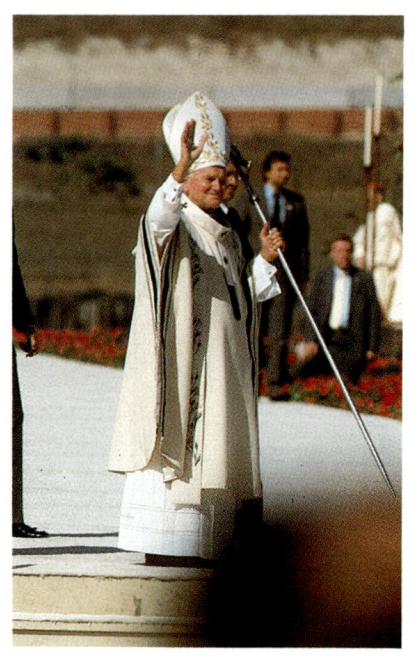

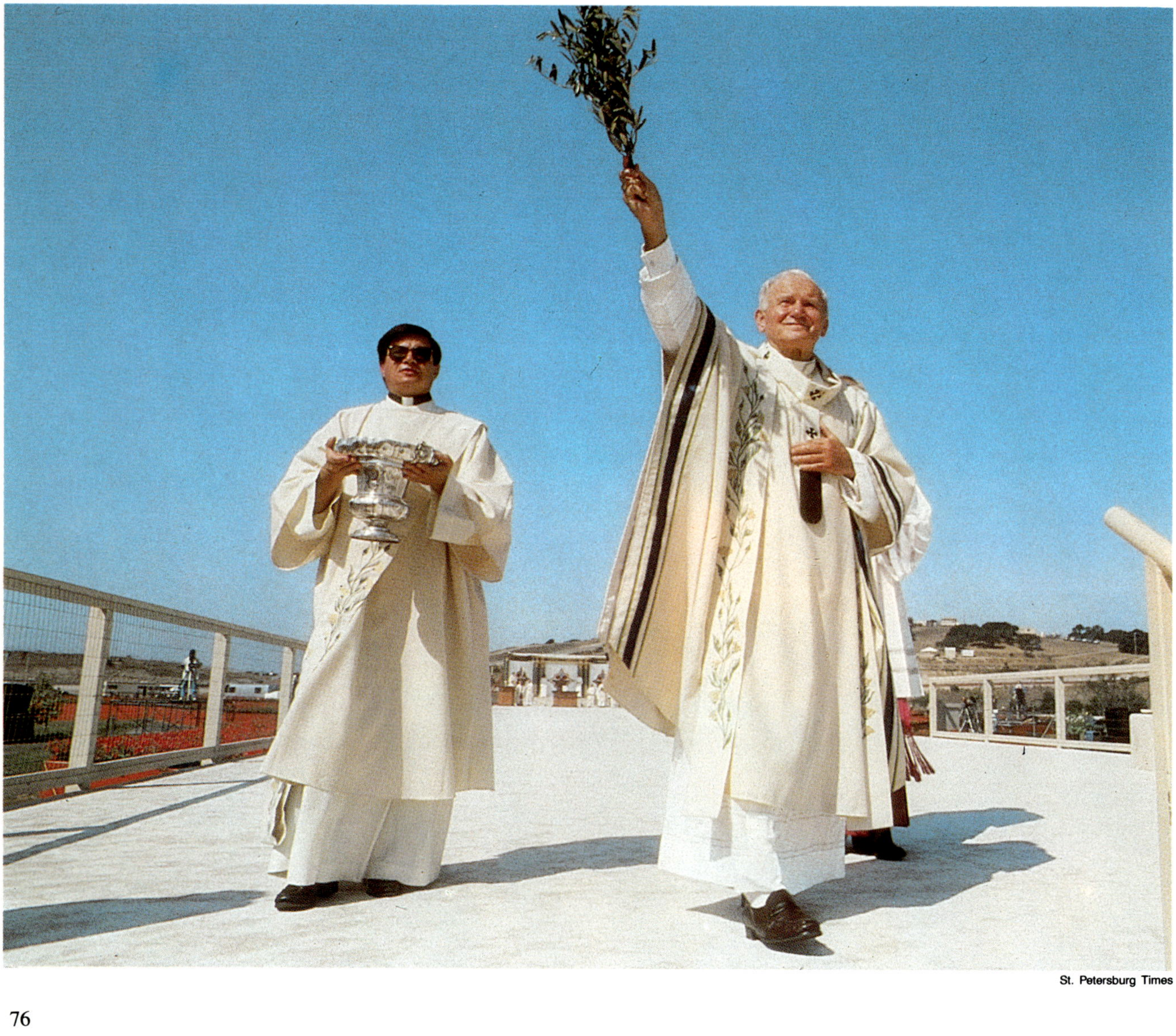

St. Petersburg Times

I ask you to join with me in praising the Most Holy Trinity for the abundance of life and goodness with which you have been gifted: "The earth has yielded its fruit. God, our God, has blessed us." But may your abundance never lead you to forget the Lord or cease to acknowledge him as the source of your peace and well-being.

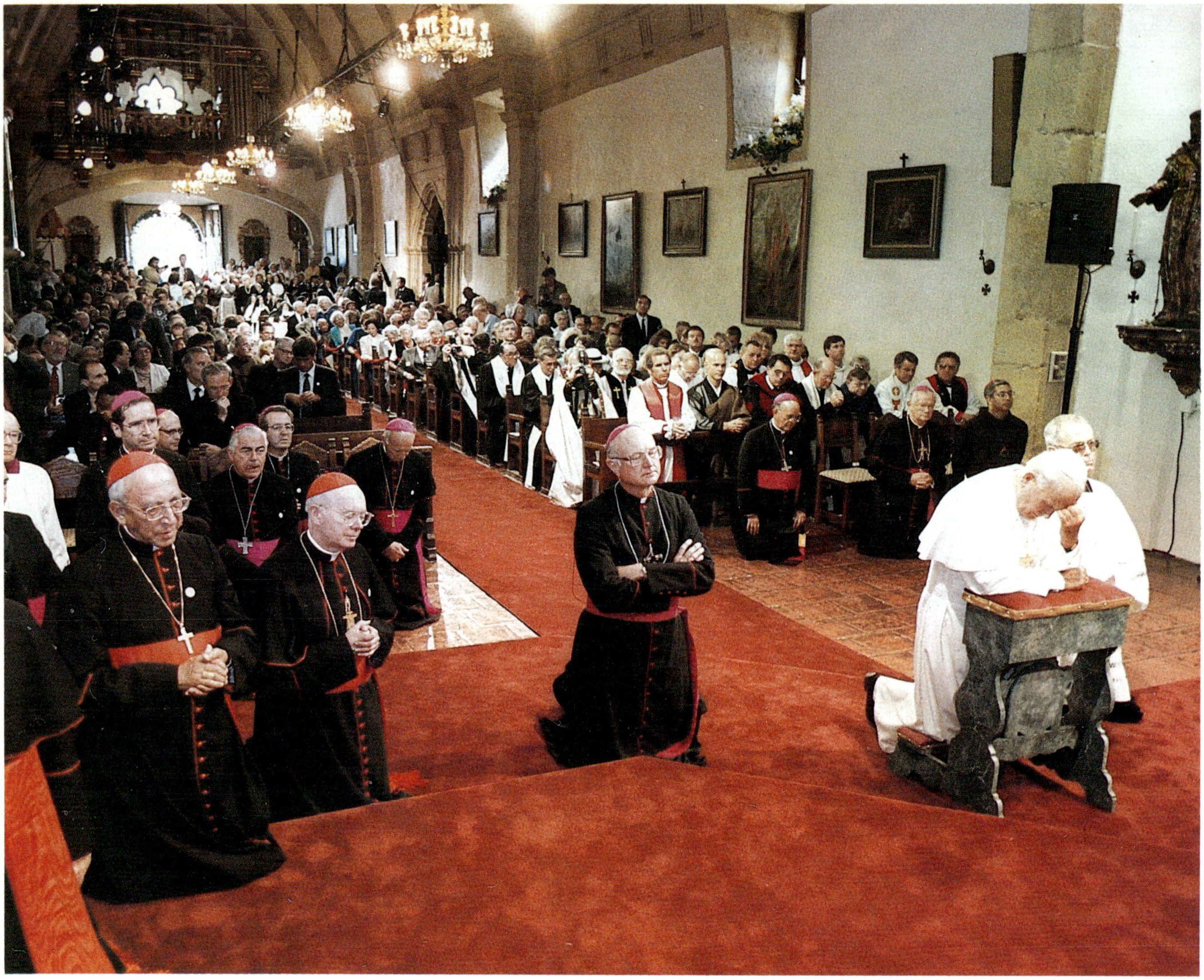

Arturo Mari

"For years to come may the Lord's face shine on this land."

Arturo Mari

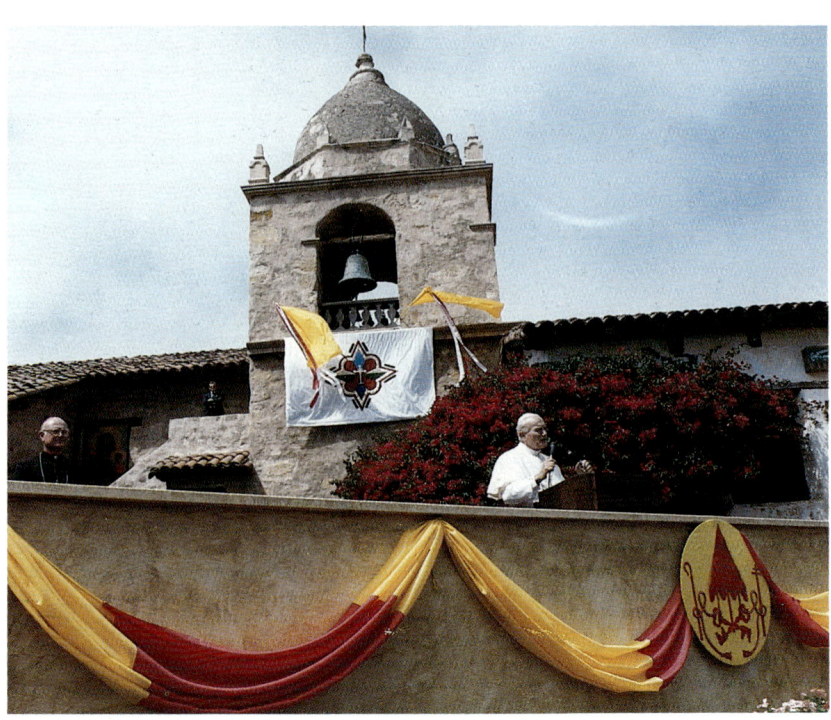

Arturo Mari

Arturo Mari

St. Petersburg Times

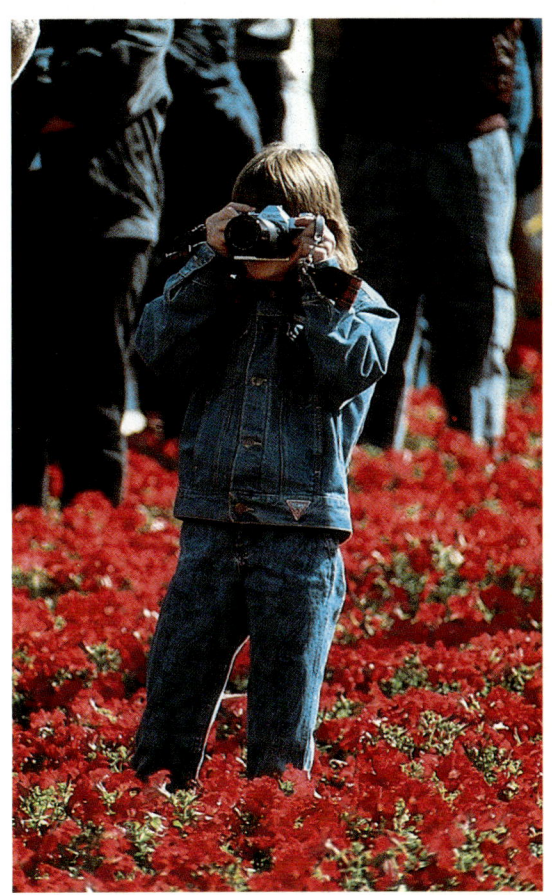

The whole of human activity must be finalized in works of justice, peace and love.

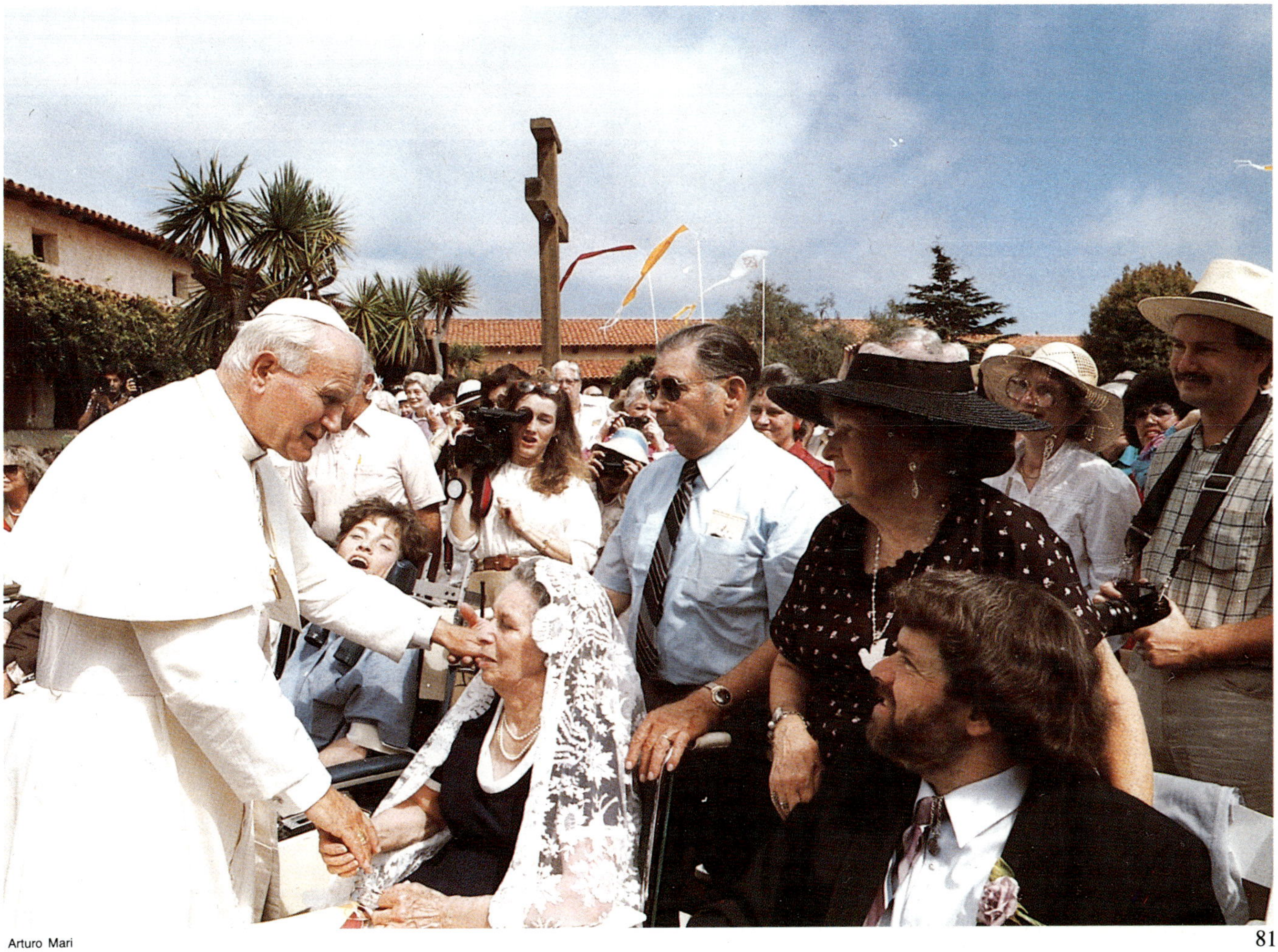

Arturo Mari

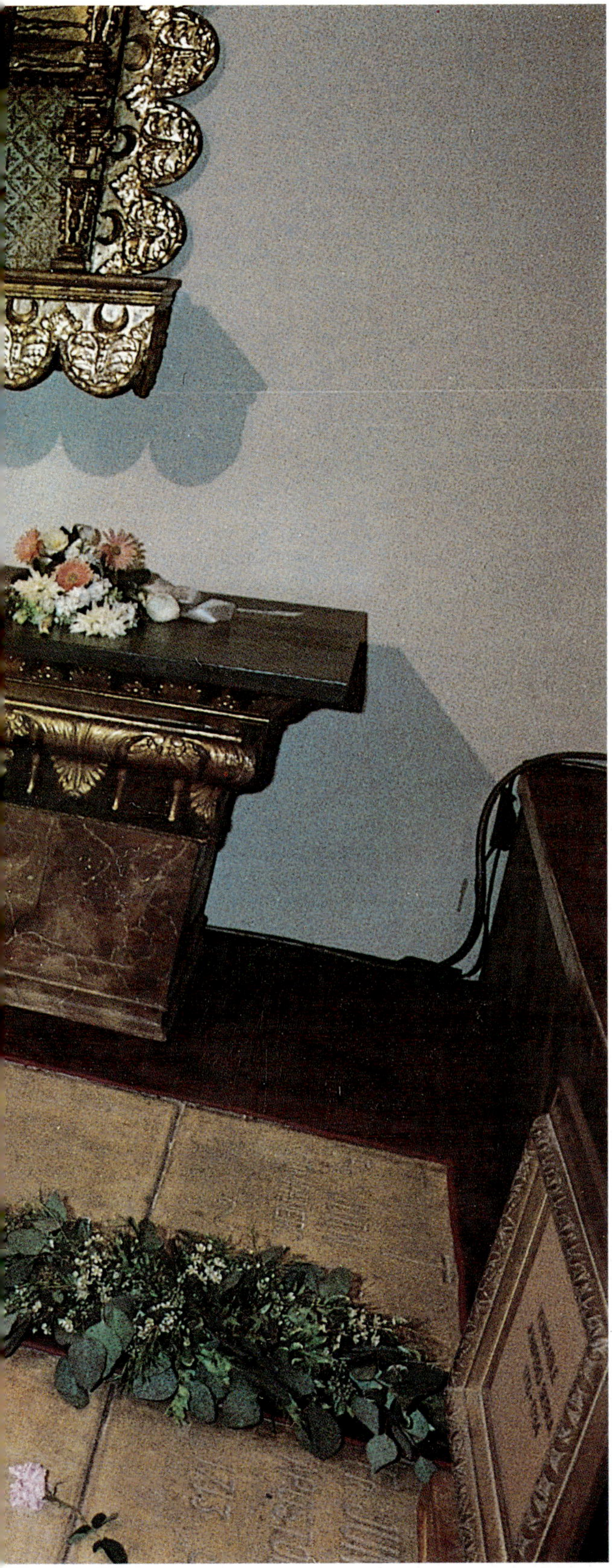

Arturo Mari

Dear brothers and sisters: like Father Serra and his Franciscan brethren, we too are called to be evangelizers, to share actively in the Church's mission of making disciples of all people.

Arturo Mari

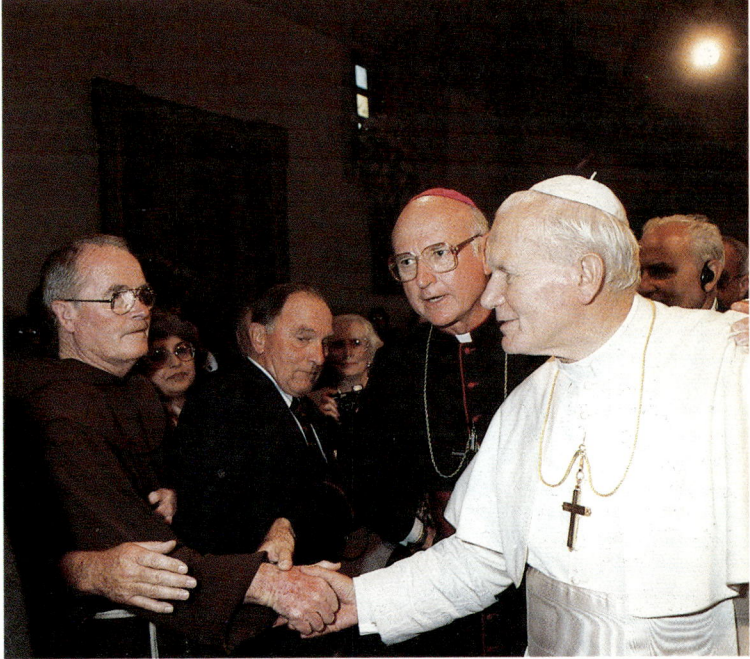

San Francisco

Dear friends in Christ: the love of God is so great that it goes beyond the limits of human language, beyond the grasp of artistic expression, beyond human understanding.

God loves you all without distinction, without limit. He loves those of you who are elderly, who feel the burden of the years. He loves those of you who are sick. He loves the relatives and friends of the sick and those who care for them. He loves us all with an unconditional and everlasting love.

In the spirit of St. Francis, then, I urge you all to open your hearts to God's love, to respond by your prayers and by the deeds of your lives. Let go of your doubts and fears, and let the mercy of God draw you to his heart. Open the doors of your hearts to our God, who is rich in mercy.

Yes, that is what we are today and forever: children of a loving God!

September 17-18, 1987

Arturo Mari

To be a Christian means to go up to the mountain to which Christ leads us, to enter into the temple of the living God that is formed in us and in our midst by the Holy Spirit. To be Christian means to continue to become Christian, learning from Christ the ways of the Lord so as to be able to "walk in his paths." To be a Christian means to become one every day, ascending spiritually toward Christ and following him. In fact, as we recall, when Christ first called those who were to become his disciples, he said to them: "Follow me."

How greatly we desire a world in which justice and peace prevail! Can the Church ever cease to proclaim the message of peace on earth? Can she ever cease to work for the true progress of peoples? Can she ever cease to work for the true dignity of every human person?

To be Christian also means to proclaim this message untiringly in every generation, in our generation at the end of the second millennium and at the threshold of the third!

St. Petersburg Times

Arturo Mari

St. Petersburg Times

Arturo Mari

The greatest challenge to the conscience of society comes from your fidelity to your own Christian vocation. It is up to you, the Catholic laity, to incarnate without ceasing the Gospel in society— in American society. You are in the forefront of the struggle to protect authentic Christian values from the onslaught of secularization. Your great contribution to the evangelization of your own society is made through your lives. Christ's message must live in you and in the way you live and in the way you refuse to live. At the same time, because your nation plays a role in the world far beyond its borders, you must be conscious of the impact of your Christian lives on others. Your lives must spread the fragrance of Christ's Gospel throughout the world.

90
DSP

DSP

Arturo Mari

91

The entire Church in the United States benefits from the dedication of American religious to their ecclesial mission.

Detroit

September 18-19, 1987

St. Petersburg Times

I feel that I must thank the Lord our God for this wonderful occasion. Detroit is a place where work, hard daily work—that privilege, duty and vocation of the human person—is a truly distinctive characteristic of urban life. This is indeed a city of workers, and very many of you here—men and women, younger people and older people, immigrants and native-born Americans—earn your living and that of your families in and around Detroit through the work of your hands, your mind, indeed your whole person. And many of you suffer from the problems that not infrequently characterize the work situation in an industrial urban setting.

This is why I would like to make reference to a subject which, as you are well aware, is close to my heart. This subject is social progress and human development in relation to the requirements of justice and to the building of a lasting peace, both in the United States and throughout the world.

Of course, dear friends, dear people of Detroit and this whole area, it is you I have primarily in mind in dealing with such a subject—you who have been created in the image and likeness of God, you who have been redeemed by the blood of the Savior, you who are children of God and brothers and sisters of Christ, you who for all of these reasons possess an incomparable dignity. But in looking at you, assembled here in Hart Plaza, I see beyond you all the people of this country and the peoples of the whole world.

Arturo Mari

The best traditions of your land presume respect for those who cannot defend themselves. If you want equal justice for all and true freedom and lasting peace, then, America, defend life!

St. Petersburg Times

Arturo Mari

This is at the very heart of the diaconate to which you have been called: to be a servant of the mysteries of Christ and, at one and the same time, to be a servant of your brothers and sisters. That these two dimensions are inseparably joined together in one reality shows the important nature of the ministry which is yours by ordination.

The service of the deacon is the Church's service sacramentalized. Yours is not just one ministry among others, but it is truly meant to be, as Paul VI described it, a "driving force" for the Church's *diaconia*. By your ordination you are configured to Christ in his servant role. You are also meant to be living signs of the servanthood of his Church.

St. Petersburg Times

Arturo Mari

St. Petersburg Times

St. Petersburg Times

99

ST. PAUL BOOK & MEDIA CENTERS OPERATED BY THE DAUGHTERS OF ST. PAUL

ALASKA
  750 West 5th Ave., Anchorage, AK 99501 **907-272-8183**.
CALIFORNIA
  3335 Motor Ave., W. Los Angeles, CA 90034 **213-202-8144**.
  1570 Fifth Ave. (at Cedar Street), San Diego, CA 92101 **619-232-1442**.
  46 Geary Street, San Francisco, CA 94108 **415-781-5180**.
CONNECTICUT
  Bridgeport: Please check your phone book for current listing.
FLORIDA
  Coral Park Shopping Center, 9808 S.W. 8 St., Miami, FL 33174 **305-559-6715; 305-559-6716**.
HAWAII
  1143 Bishop Street, Honolulu, HI 96813 **808-521-2731**.
ILLINOIS
  172 North Michigan Ave., Chicago, IL 60601 **312-346-4228; 312-346-3240**.
LOUISIANA
  423 Main Street, Baton Rouge, LA 70802 **504-343-4057; 504-336-1504**.
  4403 Veterans Memorial Blvd., Metairie, LA 70006 **504-887-7631; 504-887-0113**.
MASSACHUSETTS
  50 St. Paul's Ave., Jamaica Plain, Boston, MA 02130 **617-522-8911**.
  Rte. 1, 450 Providence Hwy, Dedham, MA 02026 **617-326-5385**.
MISSOURI
  1001 Pine Street (at North 10th), St. Louis, MO 63101 **314-621-0346**.
NEW JERSEY
  Hudson Mall, Route 440 and Communipaw Ave., Jersey City, NJ 07304 **201-433-7740**.
NEW YORK
  625 East 187th Street, Bronx, NY 10458 **212-584-0440**.
  59 East 43rd Street, New York, NY 10017 **212-986-7580**.
  78 Fort Place, Staten Island, NY 10301 **718-447-5071; 718-447-5086**.
OHIO
  616 Walnut Street, Cincinnati, OH 45202 **513-421-5733**.
  2105 Ontario Street (at Prospect Ave.), Cleveland, OH 44115 **216-621-9427**.
PENNSYLVANIA
  1719 Chestnut Street, Philadelphia, PA 19103 **215-568-2638; 215-864-0991**.
SOUTH CAROLINA
  243 King Street, Charleston, SC 29401 **803-577-0175**.
TEXAS
  114 Main Plaza, San Antonio, TX 78205 **512-224-8101**.
VIRGINIA
  1025 King Street, Alexandria, VA 22314 **703-549-3806**.
WASHINGTON
  2301 Second Ave. (at Bell), Seattle, WA 98121 **206-441-4100**.
CANADA
  3022 Dufferin Street, Toronto 395, Ontario, Canada.

Our White-clad Shepherd

Oh, John Paul II is his loved name.
Where'er he goes, the crowds acclaim
This white-clad Shepherd at whose voice—
Yes—millions thrill, exult, rejoice!

All strain to see him close at hand,
And many truly understand
That he's Christ's Vicar, teaching all,
With spirit of Saints John and Paul.

What wonders has his presence wrought
In hearts to whom he's solace brought.
Surprised were some that he would be
The one Christ chose to set them "free."

Urged on by faith, inflamed by love,
He's guided by the Lord above.
He visits lands both far and near,
Because to him God's will is dear.

With warmth and fervor, charm and grace,
With heart wide open to embrace
All those who flock to hear him speak,
He gives the truths that their minds seek.

His message rings with gentle "force."
His wisdom has no earthly source.
He radiates a love divine,
And goodness, tenderness benign.

Though John Paul II has come and gone,
His words and deeds will linger on,
Enshrined in hearts who've heard and seen
Our white-clad Shepherd, strong, serene.

—Sister Mary Paula Kolar, DSP

079060